BOYS & GIRLS
ARE
Created 2 Produce
BY
Dr. Cassandra Scott

The Fruit of the Womb is His Reward.
Psalm 127:3

DAVYNN   JAYDEN

BOYS AND GIRLS ARE CREATED2PRODUCE
BY DR. CASSANDRA SCOTT

Published
by Cassandra Scott Ministries

For ordering
information or special discounts for bulk purposes,
please contact:
Cassandra Scott Ministries
c/o Created 2 Produce
P. O. Box 841236
Pearland, Texas 77584
713.550.3370

www.Created2Produce.com
cscott@Created2Produce.com

Dr. Scott's Photographs by: Dayna Castelberg
Remember When…Photography
www.rememberwhenphoto.photoreflect.com

No part of this book may be reproduced or transmitted in any form or by any means, electronic or mechanical, including photocopy, recording, or by any information storage and retrieval system, without written permission from the author, except for the inclusion of brief quotations in a review.

ISBN: 978-0-9882936-2-5

Unless otherwise indicated, Bible quotations are taken from the HOLY BIBLE, King James Version, Public Domain.

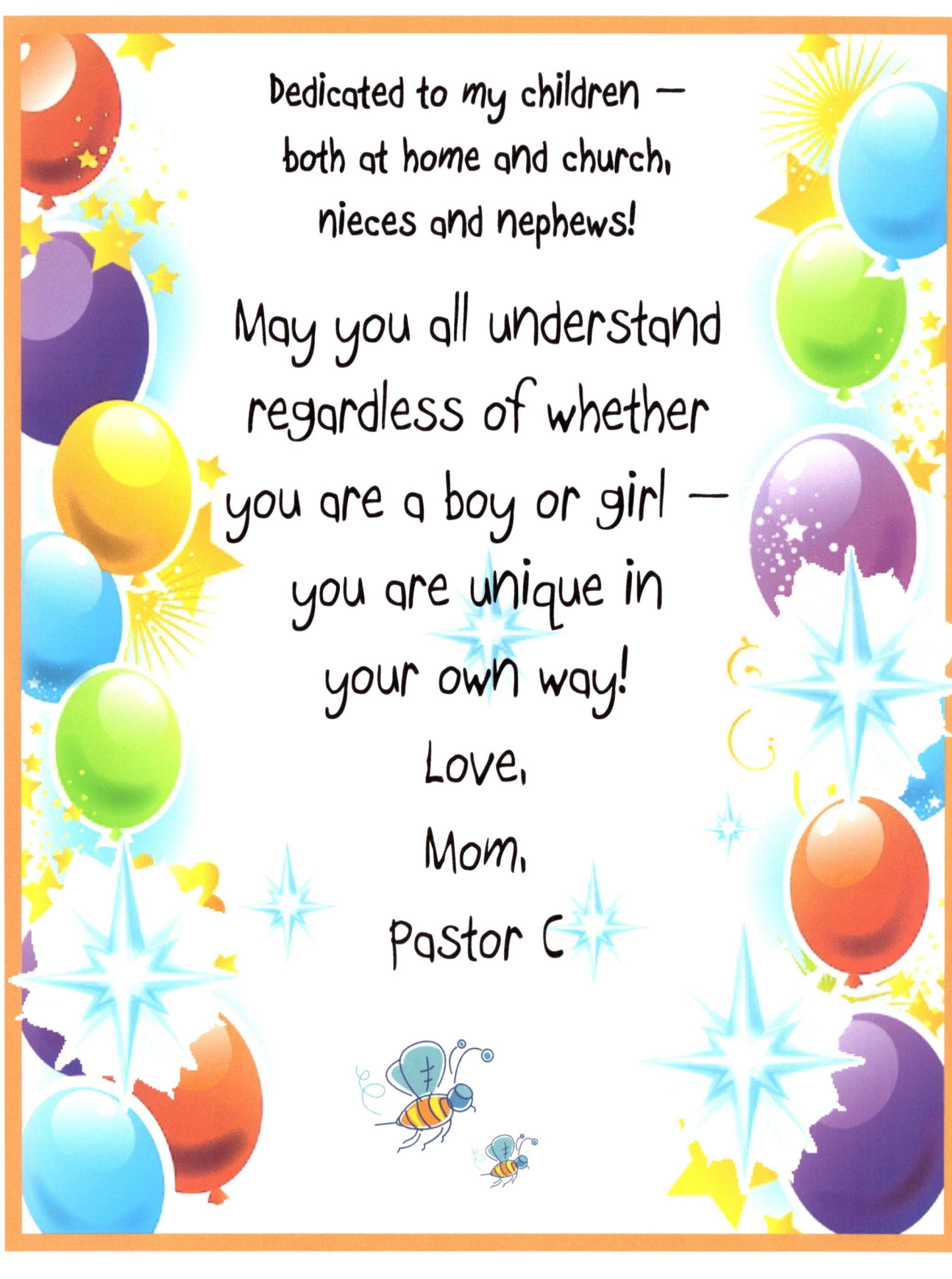

Dedicated to my children —
both at home and church,
nieces and nephews!

May you all understand regardless of whether you are a boy or girl — you are unique in your own way!

Love,

Mom,

Pastor C

When God made me

He created a masterpiece.

I am chosen for such a time as this.

I am one of a kind.

God needed me for a purpose in the earth.

Even though I have a mother and a father, *I was created in the very image of God.*

I AM CREATED2PRODUCE!

Genesis 1:27
New International Version (NIV)
So God created mankind in his own image,
in the image of God he created them;
male and female he created them.

God knew me before I ever stepped foot in the earth.

God wanted me to be who I am.

MARIA   TERESA

God knew which parents I needed, where I would live and where I would go to school.

God knew

who my friends would be, my teachers and my mentors. He even knew those who would bully me and make me cry.

I was appointed by God

to serve a group of people who will need my help. My gender was determined by Him in the beginning of time. I am Created2Produce!

Jeremiah 1:5

"Before I formed you in the womb I knew you, before you were born I set you apart; I appointed you as a prophet to the nations."

Victoria & Elizabeth

No matter how my hair, eyes, nose look.

No matter what my weight or height is…

When God created

me, He said, *"It is Good!"*

I am Created2Produce!

I am a student who is always on the Honor Roll, passing all of my classes, and having favor with all my teachers.

Wealth and riches are my covenant rights.

I have favor

with all men. I am more than a conqueror! I have the tongue of the learned. No weapon formed against me shall prosper over me or my family. God is on my side. I can do all things thru Christ which strengthens me. I shall be fruitful and multiply in all I say and do.

I am Created2Produce!

Genesis 1:28
And God blessed them, and God said unto them, Be fruitful, and multiply, and replenish the earth, and subdue it: and have dominion over the fish of the sea, and over the fowl of the air, and over every living thing that moveth upon the earth.

No matter where I go or who I meet, I will not change to please others. I will do unto others as I would have them to do unto me. I don't have to bend to peer pressure. I am happy with who I am.

I am Created2Produce!

I can use my gifts and talents to please God.

I am gifted and talented. God gave me all that I have.

My gifts will make room for me. I will end up at the right place at the right time with the right people to help me on my journey.

I am Created2Produce!

James 1:17
Every good and perfect gift is from above, coming down from the Father of the heavenly lights, who does not change like shifting shadows.

Proverbs 18:16
A man's gift makes room for him and brings him before the great.

SARAH

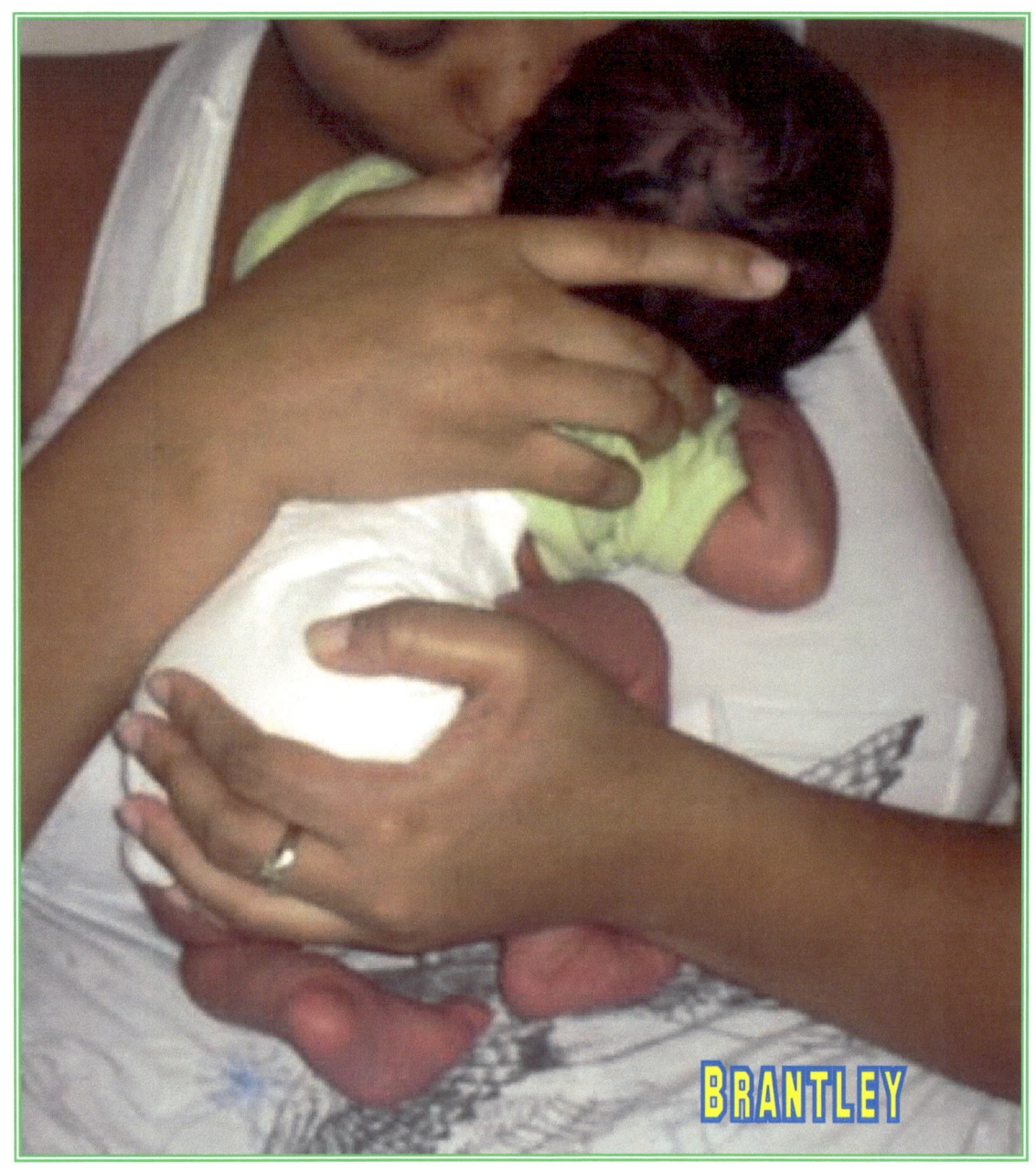

My dad and mom will show me all I need to know to be all I need to be.

God uses others too

like my teachers, aunts and uncles to help me and point me in the right direction. I will respect and honor all authority in my life. At home, school, church, or play. I am Created2Produce!

Pslams 127:4
Children born to a young man are like arrows in a warrior's hands.

There is nothing that I can think that God is not aware of. When I am happy or sad He knows. Thank you, God for making me who I am.

Whether I am a boy or a girl,
I am a great person.
I am Created2Produce!

O help me, Lord,
This day to be to be all you created me to be –
For I am Created2Produce.
Thank you for making me!!!
Amen!

NEVER FORGET

Boys & Girls
YOU
ARE
Created 2 Produce

Dr. Cassandra Scott

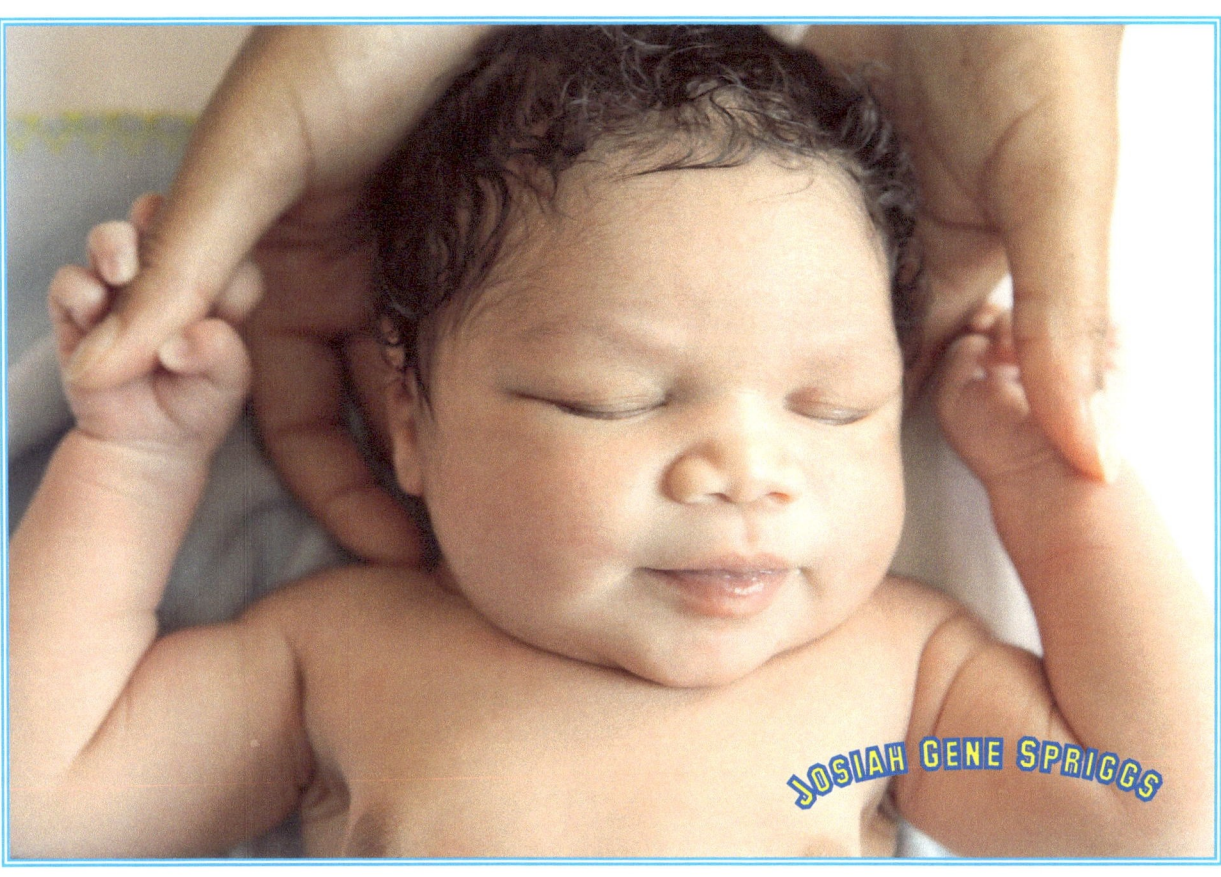

Little Josiah is the latest testimony of God at work through the ministry of Created2Produce. His parents live in Chicago. Mother, Brittany Spriggs, helps by serving administratively in Created2Produce.
(Photos and article below are reprinted with permission.)

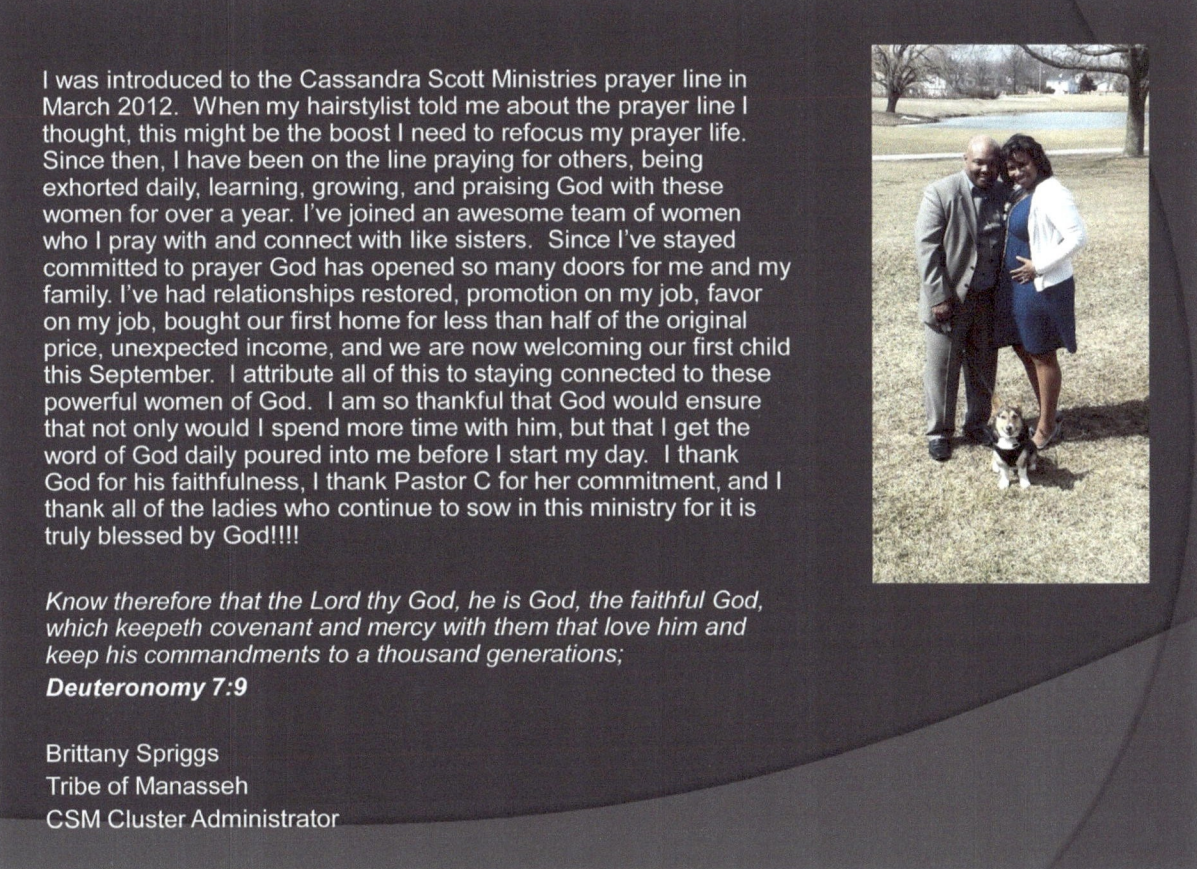

I was introduced to the Cassandra Scott Ministries prayer line in March 2012. When my hairstylist told me about the prayer line I thought, this might be the boost I need to refocus my prayer life. Since then, I have been on the line praying for others, being exhorted daily, learning, growing, and praising God with these women for over a year. I've joined an awesome team of women who I pray with and connect with like sisters. Since I've stayed committed to prayer God has opened so many doors for me and my family. I've had relationships restored, promotion on my job, favor on my job, bought our first home for less than half of the original price, unexpected income, and we are now welcoming our first child this September. I attribute all of this to staying connected to these powerful women of God. I am so thankful that God would ensure that not only would I spend more time with him, but that I get the word of God daily poured into me before I start my day. I thank God for his faithfulness, I thank Pastor C for her commitment, and I thank all of the ladies who continue to sow in this ministry for it is truly blessed by God!!!!

Know therefore that the Lord thy God, he is God, the faithful God, which keepeth covenant and mercy with them that love him and keep his commandments to a thousand generations;
Deuteronomy 7:9

Brittany Spriggs
Tribe of Manasseh
CSM Cluster Administrator

Say these Scriptures every day! Ask your parents to help you copy and post them in a safe place so you can see and remember them.

Sons are a heritage from the LORD, children a reward from him. Like arrows in the hands of a warrior are sons born in one's youth. Blessed is the man whose quiver is full of them. They will not be put to shame when they contend with their enemies in the gate. Psalms 127:3-5

Then Esau looked up and saw the women and children. "Who are these with you?" he asked. Jacob answered, "They are the children God has graciously given your servant." Genesis 33:5

He settles the barren woman in her home as a happy mother of children. Praise the LORD. Psalm 113:9

But as for you, continue in what you have learned and have become convinced of, because you know those from whom you learned it, and how from infancy you have known the holy Scriptures, which are able to make you wise for salvation through faith in Christ Jesus. 2 Timothy 3:14-15

Like newborn babies, crave pure spiritual milk, so that by it you may grow up in your salvation, now that you have tasted that the Lord is good. 1 Peter 2:2-3

People were bringing little children to Jesus to have him touch them, but the disciples rebuked them. When Jesus saw this, he was indignant. He said to them, "Let the little children come to me, and do not hinder them, for the kingdom of God belongs to such as these. I tell you the truth, anyone who will not receive the kingdom of God like a little child will never enter it." And he took the children in his arms, put his hands on them and blessed them. Mark 10:13-16

Train a child in the way he should go, and when he is old he will not turn from it.
Proverbs 22:6

Folly is bound up in the heart of a child, but the rod of discipline will drive it far from him.
Proverbs 22:15

Impress them on your children. Talk about them when you sit at home and when you walk along the road, when you lie down and when you get up. Deuteronomy 6:7

Children, obey your parents in the Lord, for this is right. "Honor your father and mother"--which is the first commandment with a promise - "that it may go well with you and that you may enjoy long life on the earth." Fathers, do not exasperate your children; instead, bring them up in the training and instruction of the Lord.
Ephesians 6:1-4

Honor your father and your mother, so that you may live long in the land the LORD your God is giving you. Exodus 20:12

Listen, my son, to your father's instruction and do not forsake your mother's teaching. They will be a garland to grace your head and a chain to adorn your neck. Proverbs 1:8-9

You shall not bow down to them or worship them; for I, the LORD your God, am a jealous God, punishing the children for the sin of the fathers to the third and fourth generation of those who hate me, but showing love to a thousand [generations] of those who love me and keep my commandments. Exodus 20:5-6

Teach them to your children, talking about them when you sit at home and when you walk along the road, when you lie down and when you get up. Deuteronomy 11:19

He took a little child and had him stand among them. Taking him in his arms, he said to them, "Whoever welcomes one of these little children in my name welcomes me; and whoever welcomes me does not welcome me but the one who sent me." Mark 9:36-37

Children, obey your parents in everything, for this pleases the Lord. Colossians 3:20